FLY

Kenneth David Brubacher

FLY

AuthorHouse™
1663 Liberty Drive
Bloomington, IN 47403
www.authorhouse.com
Phone: 1 (800) 839-8640

Illustrations by Eric Smith / IronMedia.ca

A Hat & Hammer Production
A Division of Brubacher Technologies Ltd.
Visit: hat&hammerproductions.com

Made in Canada

Published by AuthorHouse 11/21/2015

ISBN: 978-1-5049-5353-5 (sc)
ISBN: 978-1-5049-5354-2 (e)
ISBN: 978-1-5049-5355-9 (hc)

Library of Congress Control Number: 2015916084

Print information available on the last page.

authorHOUSE®

ALSO BY KENNETH DAVID BRUBACHER

The Watcher

The Poor Shoemaker

Mennonite Cobbler

There’s An Angel Under My Bed

Commotion in the ManureYard

Leafy and Sprucy

Fire Dragon Moon

The Book of Truth and Wisdom

Amos and Salina Go To Town

This book is for

Elyse Rose Hiller

My Granddaughter

A Delightful Young Lady

There is a Fly in my Truck

It

Buzzez around

Inside my Truck

Buzz Buzz Buzzzz

There is a Fly in my Truck

Yes Fly is still there

I know Fly is still there

I can see Fly And I can hear Fly Buzz

Buzz Buzz Buzzzz

Sometimes Fly Buzzez around

But sometimes Fly just sits there

That Buzzing Fly is still in my Truck

I cannot catch Fly

I would like to catch Fly because Fly

Buzzezez ezzz

Into small places   Where I cannot go

Fly can go into small places

Because Fly is small

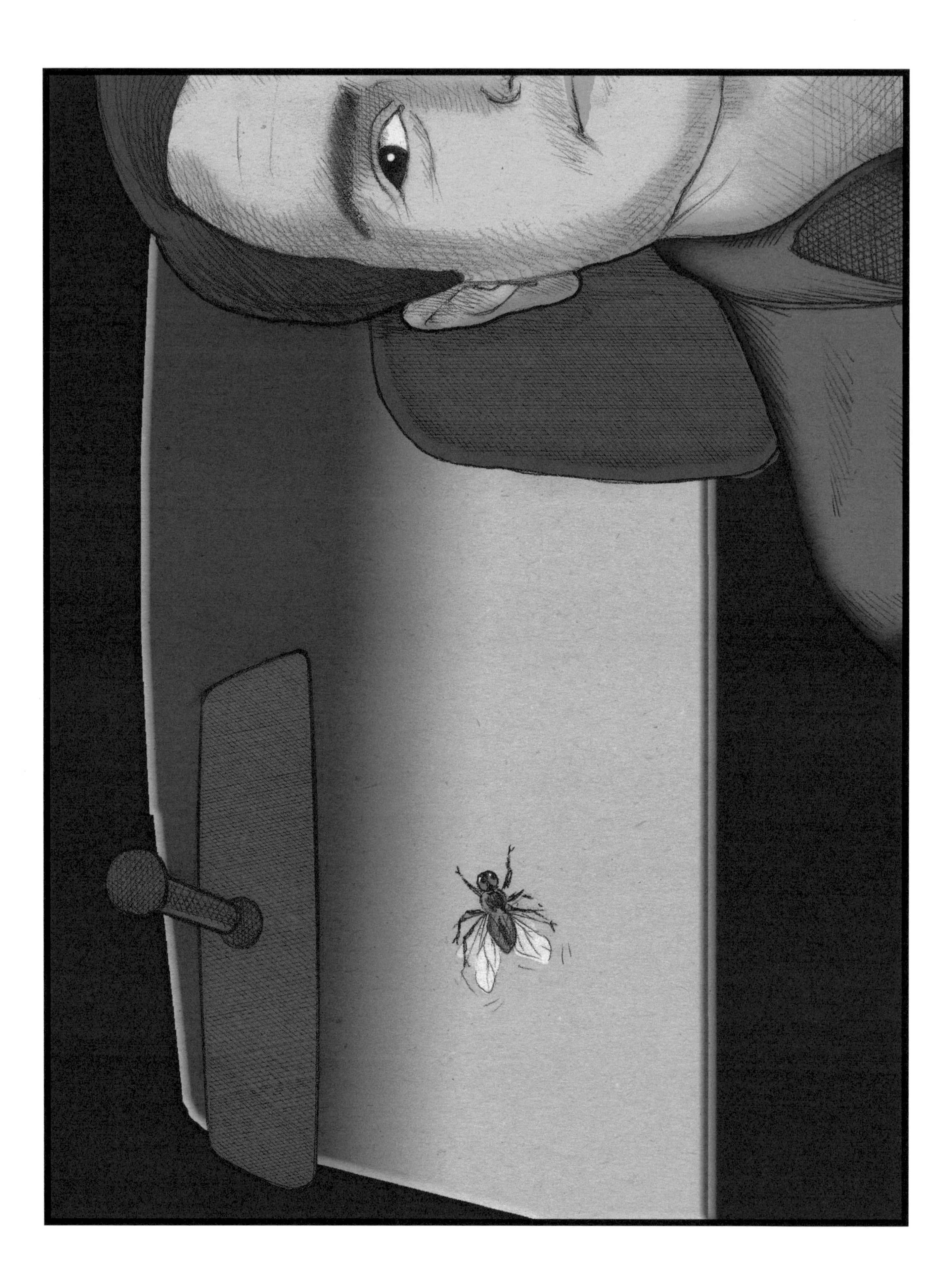

Yes

You are right

Fly is still in my Truck

It is a Chevy Silverado

The Truck

Not the Fly

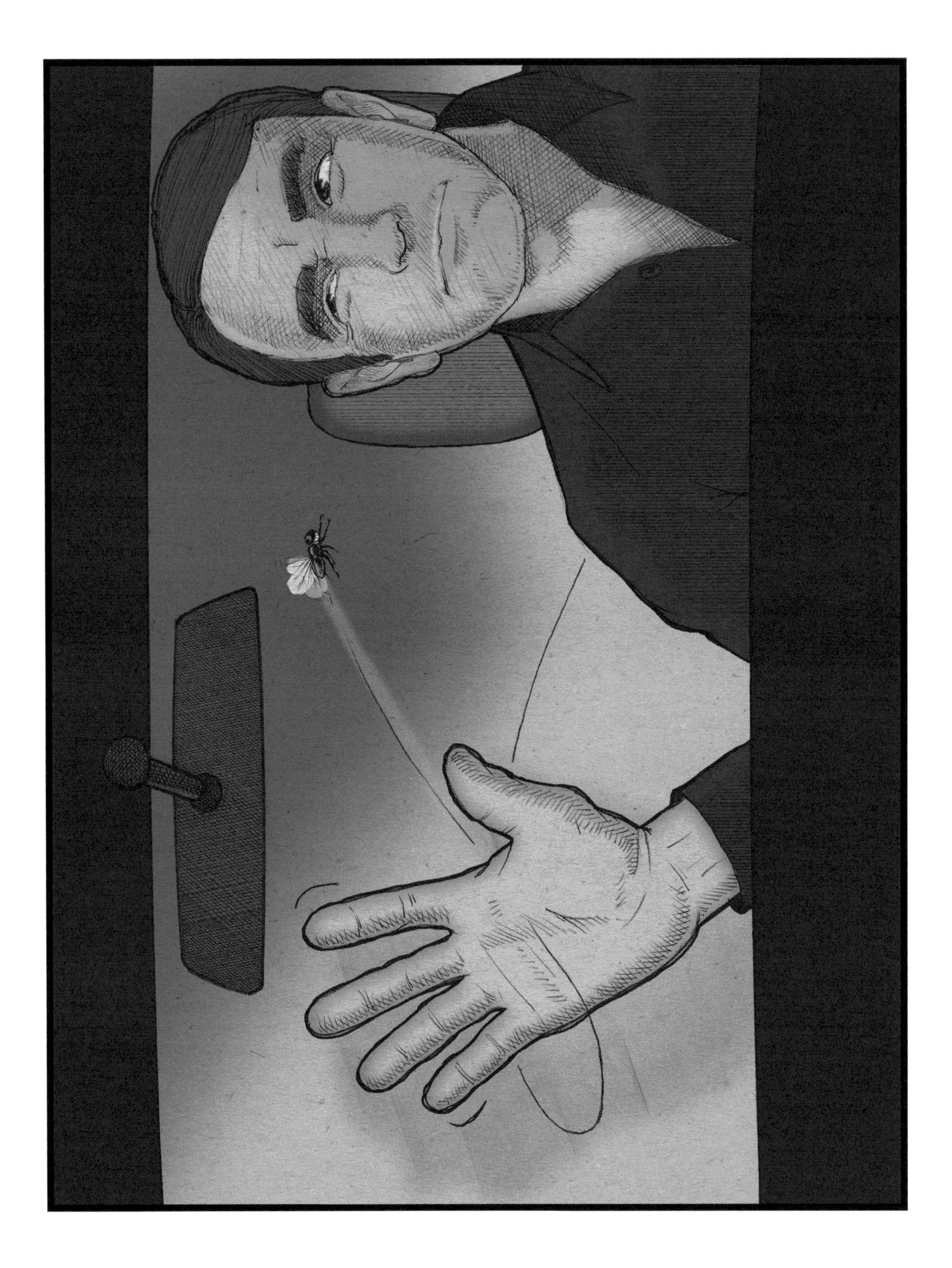

When Chevy is sitting still

I try to catch Fly

But Fly knows

Fly knows I am trying to catch Fly

And then Fly goes and hides

Sometimes Fly goes and hides

Under the front seat of Chevy

I try to reach under the front seat

And find Fly there

But when I get close   Fly Buzzez Off

And hides in another place

Sometimes Fly finds another place

And sits very still

Then I cannot find Fly

Like on the window

On the far side of Chevy

Fly walks across the window

And stops to look at me

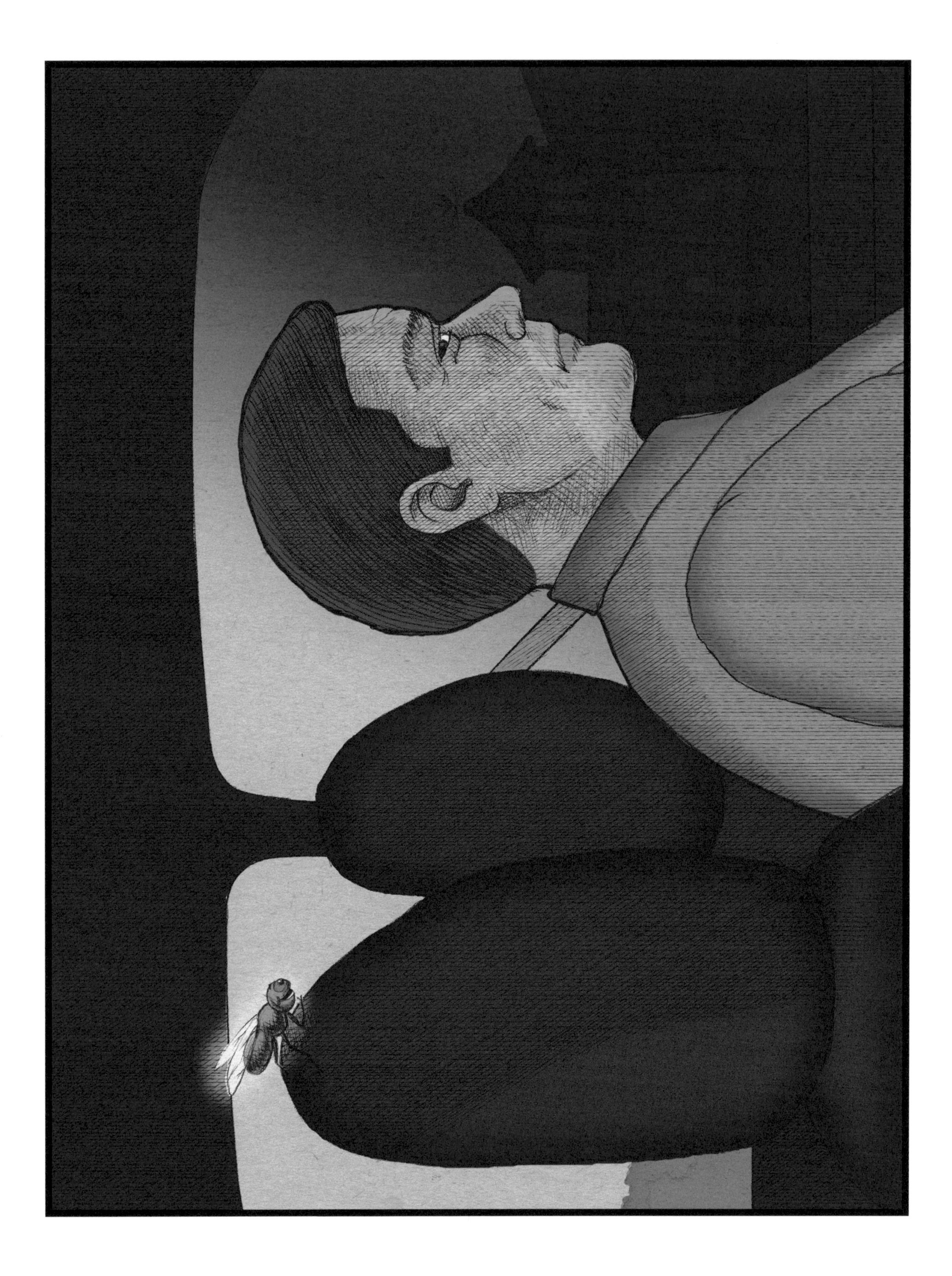

Mostly Fly is either Buzzing

Or is very quiet

And yet when I listen very carefully

I think maybe I can hear Fly talking to me

I think Fly might be saying

You cannot catch me

Fly says this in Fly language

I think   Maybe

The Fly in my truck

Likes to Buzz around

While I am driving

Fly likes to Buzz around at the windows

Sometimes Fly Buzzez at the back window

Or sometimes on the side windows

But most often

Fly Buzzez at the window in front of me

While I am driving

Fly is teasing me because

I might well be able to catch Fly

But I am not allowed to try

While I am driving

Fly

Drives me crazy when I am driving

Because the laws of driving

Will send People in Hats to put me in jail

If I try to catch Fly when I am driving

I do not want to go to jail

So I do not try to catch Fly when I drive

I park Chevy beside my house

And open the doors

I will chase Fly out of Chevy

But first I have to find Fly

There

Fly is under the seat on the far side

Fly is looking at me from under the seat

Now I know what to do

I take the snow brush with the long handle

And push it over at Fly

Who is hiding under the seat

It works

Fly flies away Out of Chevy

Into my house

There is a Fly in my house

It Buzzez around

Buzz Buzz Buzzzzz

And more Buzz

I cannot catch Fly

Fly buzzes onto places I cannot go

At first

Fly Buzzez into the mud room

This is where my coats and boots are

There are lots of places there for Fly to hide

Fly finds a lot of these places

Behind my coats and boots

Where I cannot catch Fly

When I move the coats to one side

Fly goes into the kitchen

There Fly finds lots of fun places to hide

Fly hides behind the stove

And then Fly hides behind the fridge

In between hiding

Fly Buzzez around the kitchen

Buzz BuzzBuzz Buzzzzz

Then

Fly goes into the living room

Fly likes it in the living room

Fly Buzzez around the windows

And then Fly stops on the ceiling

Fly walks around on the ceiling

Where I cannot go

Fly stops and looks at me

Fly looks at me and I think

Maybe I can see Fly blink

I am not sure but I think

Fly also talks to me

If I stop to listen

I can learn what Fly is telling me

Yes

I am Fly

I am up here   Looking down on you

You are very big and very strong

I am very small

And I am not strong at all

You could swat me like a fly

But I can fly   I can really fly

I fly

Therefore   I am

Fly

You can only *dream* of flying

Flying in your dreams

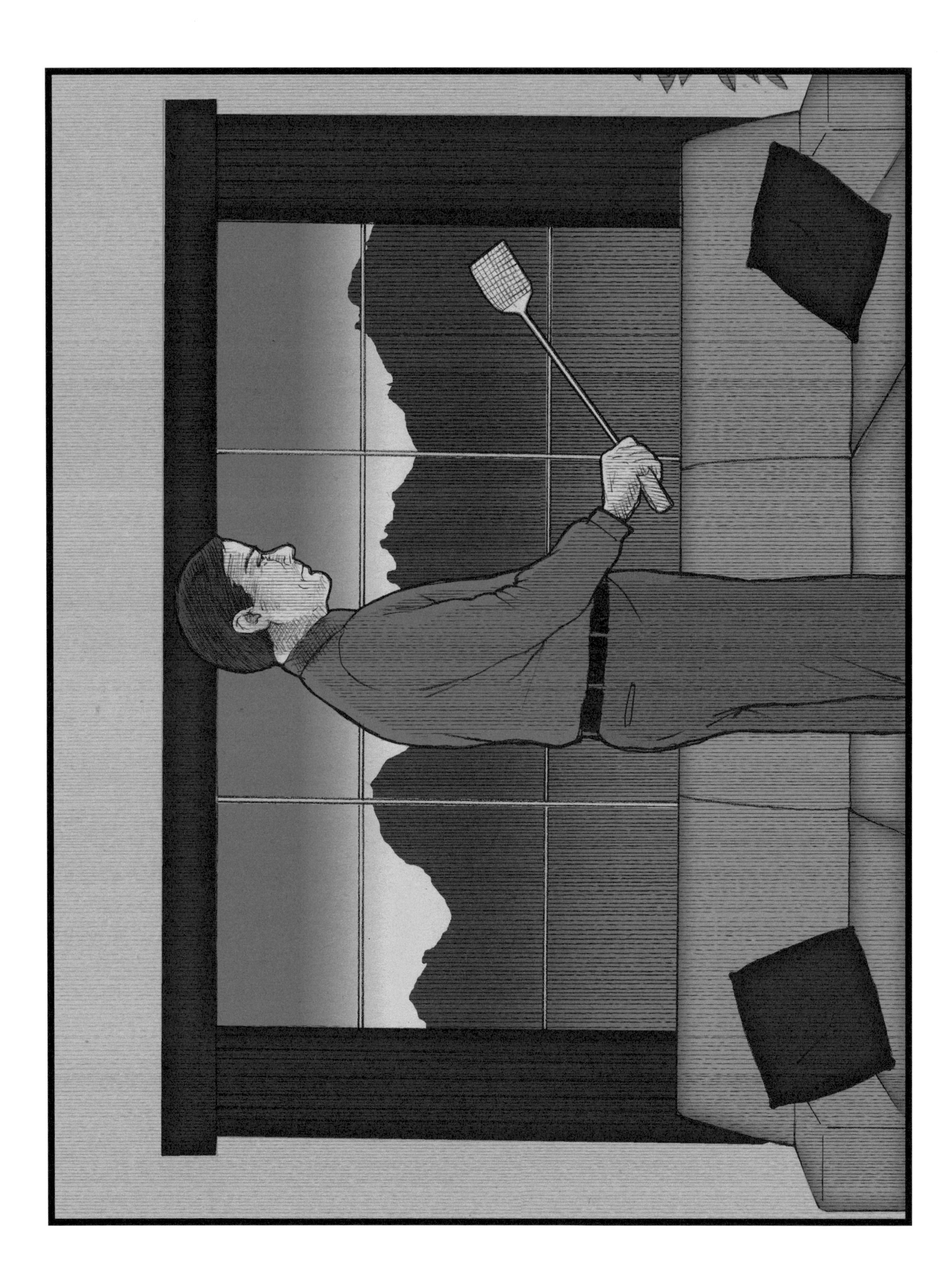

The fly swatter is in my hand

But I cannot swat Fly

I cannot hurt Fly

Fly is only doing here

What Flies are meant to do

The life of Fly is short

So let Fly Fly

Flights beauty is in Flight

We all Dream of Flying

Yes Dream

But if we close our eyes

And look to the Sun

Maybe we could also Fly

Really Fly Let go and Fly

Mayhap there be True Joy in Flight

The door to the kitchen is open

The door to the mudroom is open

The door to the house is open

And out flies Fly

Into the Spring sunshine

To Fly with others that Fly

Really ***Fly***

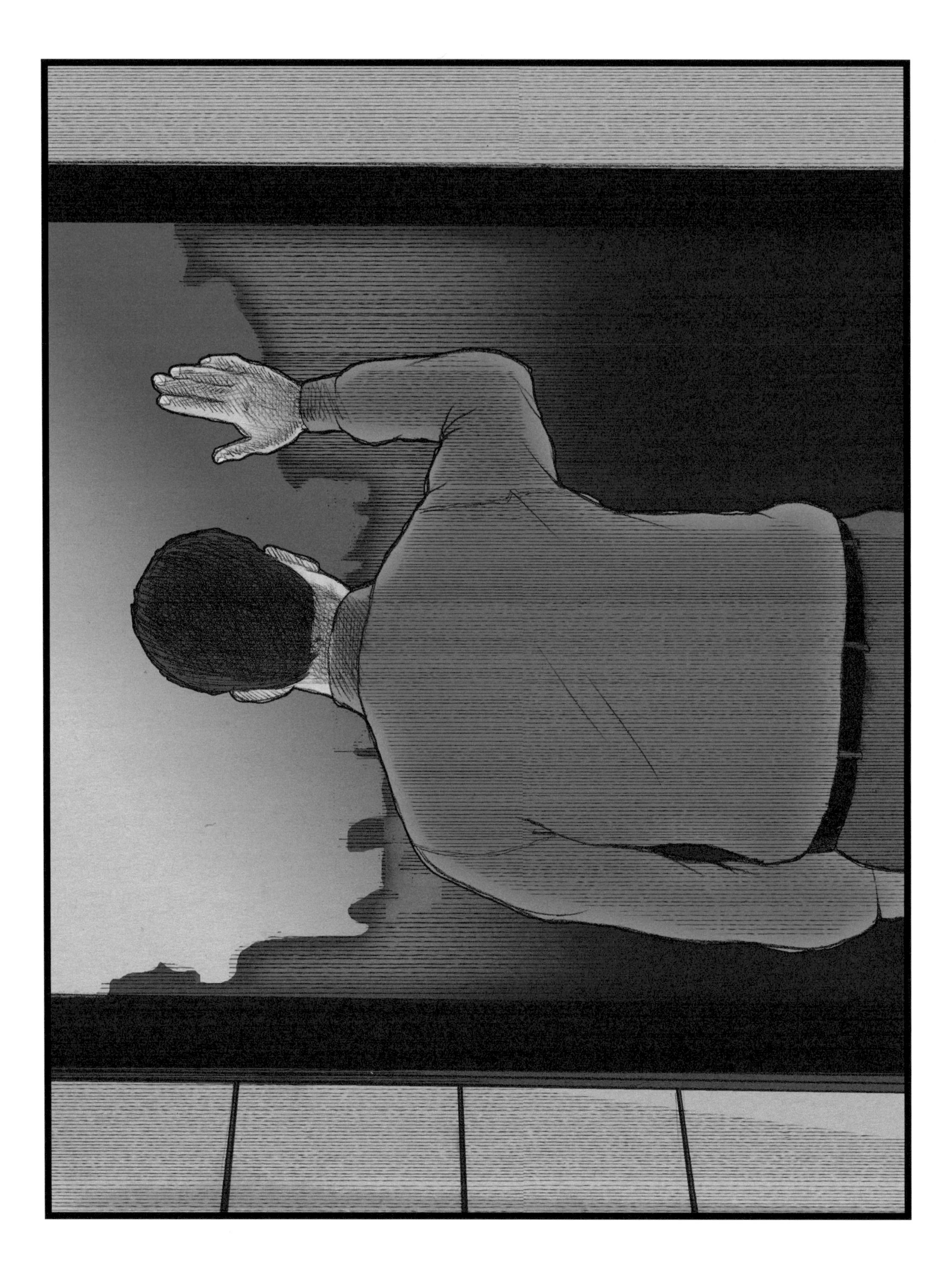

Bye   Fly

Bye Bye Fly

May Flight of Dreams

Be ever with us

Maybe   Just beyond our pillows

Guide tonight our dreamy Flight

Or

Maybe this is just a FlyBy

Maybe all a Dream

About the Author

Kenneth David Brubacher was born into a large family of sort of Mennonites in Elmira, ON, through no fault of his own. He was encouraged to make an attempt at becoming a normal human being, but clearly with limited success. To the surprise of nearly everyone he graduated from secondary school in 1970.

From there he traveled the world extensively, turning his hand to many kinds of jobs, and eventually returned to Elmira having accomplished very little. He got work as a millwright, but it was soon evident that he was a millwrong. After being mercifully fired from that job he went trucking and almost immediately distinguished himself (Summa Cum Laude with Oak Leaf Cluster and Silver Star) by destroying the truck.

He married and begat two lovely daughters who took after their mother in many wonderful ways, and turned out normal. It was considered a blessing that he had no sons because there was a high degree of probability that they might well grow up to be like their dad.

Knowing little about shoes, and even less about feet, he then took over his father's shoe repair shop and started to make shoes by hand along about April Fools' Day 1978. Very few people caught on. It was obvious that people whose feet were so bad that they sought out the services of a cobbler were not very fussy. The business prospered in spite of its inherent inadequacies.

He also applied himself to many varieties of sport, establishing a universal mediocrity in their pursuit seldom seen. When his body was sufficiently trashed he took up umpiring baseball, where it was observed that his training must have occurred under the tender administrations of the CNIB.

Currently he makes his home on a rented farm near Creemore, ON, and repairs a few shoes in his small shop in Collingwood. The farmhouse will soon become a gravel pit, whereupon it was his intent to establish institutions where Mennonites could go to seek quiet enjoyment. This, of course, until it was pointed out to him that they had already done it. These establishments are known as Mennonite Farms.

The author heartily recommends that any reader who takes a notion to write and produce a book or a play, then to lie down on the couch and watch videos of fawns gamboling in a sun-splashed meadow full of butterflies - until the feeling goes away.

It is hoped that you enjoy the book, and that its contents and presentation may provide therapeutic assistance in the remedy of your insomnia.

Printed in the United States
By Bookmasters